In Search of a Face

In Search of a Face

Aurélia Lassaque

Translated by Madeleine Campbell

WHITE PINE PRESS / BUFFALO, NEW YORK

White Pine Press
P.O. Box 236
Buffalo, NY 14201
www.whitepine.org

Publication of this book was supported by public funds from the New York State Council on the Arts, with the support of Governor Kathy Hochul and the New York State Legislature, a State Agency.

Acknowledgements: See page 147.

Printed and bound in the United States of America.

ISBN 978-1-945680-81-6

Library of Congress Control Number: 2024939693

In Search of a Face

Foreword

Aurélia Lassaque (b. 1983) is a bilingual poet who composes in French and Occitan. Endangered today, Occitan, the language of the medieval Troubadours, considered to be the fathers of Euroopean lyricism, is still spoken in Southern France, in Val d'Aran (Spain) and in a few valleys in the Piedmont region of Italy.

Aurélia dedicated her doctoral dissertation to 17th century Occitan theatre. She often collaborates with visual and video artists, dancers and particularly musicians and accompanies her readings with short songs from the Occitan folklore tradition. She has performed in Europe and Scandinavia, North Africa, Latin America, India, Indonesia and Taiwan. An active advocate of linguistic diversity, she acts as literary advisor for the Paroles Indigo festival in Arles and the Premio Ostana Scritture in Lingua Madre (Italy). She was nominated in 2016 by the Printemps des poètes to join the European poetry platform Versopolis, where her chapbooks have appeared in Lithuanian, Polish, Macedonian, Italian and Georgian

Aurélia Lassaque's first bilingual poetry collection *Pour que chantent les salamandres*, published by Editions Bruno Doucey, has been translated into English, Dutch, Norwegian, Hebrew, Catalan, German and Spanish and received critical attention from, among others, *The Guardian*, the literary supplement of *Al Araby Al Jadeed* and *Haaretz Daily*: "In her works Occitan and French marry, complete each other, hold a dialogue. [...] Her poetry oscillates not only between two languages, but between two worlds. She unveils what is universal in the language of intimacy. She deals in timeless subjects within a form that is invariably contemporary." (Amir Beker, *Haaretz Daily,* March 4, 2015).

Her editor, Bruno Doucey, wrote of Aurélia Lassaque's first bilingual collection: "A young lady whose writing day began thousands of years ago [...], she writes in two different languages but speaks with one single voice, so much is her poetry conceived to be voiced, sung, danced. In Mexico, in Brazil, in the whole wide Amerindian world, Aurélia Lassaque would be something of a shaman; her readers would approach her poems as one might gather wild plants to heal oneself or fend off a curse [...]. Aurélia Lassaque, faithful to the happy rumor of childhood, invites us to pagan feasts, primitive ring-dances, rustic fantasmagories in which two stories always mingle — one old, the other contemporary."

Her poems have appeared in translation in numerous magazines and anthologies. Her second French/Occitan collection, *En quête d'un visage* was published in France by Editions Bruno Doucey (May 2017) and funded by the C.R.L. Midi-Pyrénées. The translator, Madeleine Campbell, was sponsored in Fall 2017 by the Emerging Translators Program of the American Literary Translators Association (ALTA) to complete its translation into English under the mentorship of Steve Bradbury.

Aurélia Lassaque first performed Campbell's translations from *En quête d'un visage* in Rotterdam at Poetry International (2018) and selected translations from this collection have since been published in the U.K. in *Poems from the Edge of Extinction* (2019) and in the U.S.A. in *The Arkansas International* (2020).

En quête d'un visage (*In Search of a Face*) rewrites Homer's ancient myth through a dialogue between Ulysses and Elle/Ela (She). Originally written in French and Occitan, this timeless narrative poem rewrites Homer's tale from the perspective of the one who is left to wait. Explaining why Elle/Ela (She) has no name, author Aurélia Lassaque tells us "her name is unknown, for her story has been subsumed in his story and the rewritings of history." But although 'She' has no name, Aurélia gives her a voice in Occitan, through which we re-encounter Homer's tale from the perspective of two lovers driven apart by fate. An echo of formal Greek poïesis, at a time before drama, song and poetry were separated, this text was conceived as much for the stage as for the page. It comprises eight Cantos with prose poems in Occitan, while a third voice adopts in French the role of the chorus in ancient classical drama.

While Ulysses roams the seas, 'She' roams the territory of her memory, grapples with its impostor nostalgia, is driven to the brink of madness by the relentless materiality of absence, age and regret. Time is stretched by waiting in perpetuum for her lover's return in the rarefied echo chamber of Elle/Ela's memory, while elements of space are sparsely sketched out, as in a dream. The theme of memory is employed here to stage the prison in which 'She' is detained, in the shadow of the myth:

serai aquí, i aurà lo miralh

e parlarem de tu, ieu e l'autra al dedins del miralh

la rejonharai aquí, sempre de galís, al ras d'una cadièra,
al biais dels aucèls

*

i'll be here, the mirror, there

and we'll speak of you, i and the other in the mirror

i'll join her there, always a little slant, on the edge of a chair,
the way birds do

This poignant re-interpretation of an archetypal story, at once highly intimate and universal in its reach, explores the toll that war and separation take on those who leave and those who are left behind: "Dona-me un nom, Ulisses/dona-me un nom que te posquèsse esperar" (Give me a name, Ulysses/give me a name so that i can wait for you).

En quête d'un visage addresses perennial themes of love and abandonment, war and separation, and the loss of identity they engender through a gifted poet and a major voice in Occitan contemporary poetry. It is entirely apposite that Aurélia Lassaque should do so through the medium of Occitan, a language that is, like the 'She' recreated by the poet from the perspective of the nameless woman, in danger of being forgotten in the shadow of a global world dominated by global languages.

Prologue

Elle

Tout ceci est de mémoire profane

les poètes ont tout réinventé

il fallait un homme
qui surpasse les dieux
et qui comme tout homme
loin de sa maison
si souvent en larmes
maudisse la mer vineuse
se griffe le visage

quand le poète est mort
dix autres ont pris sa place et ont récrit l'histoire

ainsi l'homme a engendré le mythe

She

The tale that follows is from profane memory

the poets reinvented everything

they needed a man
to upstage the gods
and, like any man
far from home
with much weeping
to curse the wine-dark sea
and tear at his face

when the poet died
ten others took his place and rewrote the story

and so man created the myth

J'ai cloué l'espoir aux quatre murs de ma cellule

il n'est pas de territoire plus vaste que celui de ma mémoire
j'ai creusé ses montagnes, vidé ses rivières
retourné les pierres de toutes ses murailles
en attendant le retour de mon amant barbare

cet homme qui rassemble vos voix
endure vos délires
et porte tous les masques

cet homme que vous appelez Ulysse

i nailed hope to the four walls of my cell

there is no land more vast than memory
i hollowed out its mountains, drained its rivers
turned over the stones of every rampart
waiting for my errant lover's return

the man who rallies your voices
endures your deliriums
and wears every mask

the man you call Ulysses

Chant I

Le soleil s'est levé. Le garçon lui murmure ses commandements.

Non loin de lui est agenouillée celle qu'il aime. Les bras enfouis dans le sable, elle creuse.
Le garçon prie : que l'on se souvienne de son nom, que l'on s'en souvienne jusqu'au dernier homme, qu'Ulysse soit le dernier homme.
Puis il saisit le soleil à pleines mains, le mord et le crible de rire.

Elle n'a pas besoin d'entendre ses prières pour savoir de quoi sont faits les rêves d'Ulysse.
Alors elle creuse à la manière d'un animal que l'orage rend furieux.
Un labyrinthe. Elle voudrait pouvoir y retenir le soleil, que la mer soit complice.
Elle y dépose de petites statues d'argile.
Une pour elle, une pour Ulysse.
Ils se tiennent par la main.
Il y a une noce.

Mais le labyrinthe est de sable.
Chaque matin, il faut tout recommencer et quand vient l'heure de la noce, elle jure deux fois.

Canto I

The sun has risen. Facing it, the boy murmurs his commandments.

Close by, kneeling, is the one he loves. Arm-deep in sand, she digs.
The boy prays: that they may remember his name, that they remember his name until the last man, that Ulysses be that man.
After, he grabs the sun with both hands, takes a bite and riddles it with laughter.

She has no need to hear his prayers, she knows what Ulysses' dreams are made of.
And so she burrows like an animal maddened by storm.
A labyrinth. She wishes she could hold the sun there, make the sea her accomplice.
In the labyrinth she places small statues of clay.
One for herself, one for Ulysses.
Their hands are clasped.
A wedding is held.

But the labyrinth is made of sand.
Every morning, she must begin again and come the wedding hour,
she vows twice over.

Ela

L'iscla serva las regas
dels rires baujes
de dròlles venguts del larg

a l'ombra dels taulièrs
m'ensenhavas tos juòcs
aviam pas dètz ans
e carrejavas de tresaurs
dins tas pòchas traucadas

als aujòls de la riba
panavas de fials
per i passar de pèiras
en forma d'arcèli

los peisses èran bòrnis
e la frucha tròp amara
que pausavas tremolant
a l'abroa de ma fenèstra

l'olivièr aviá un nom
que t'aviái fisat
tant coma l'alfabet
que s'engrava al frejal
sus l'arbre mèstre de las naus

She

This island is scarred
with shrieks of laughter
from children of the high seas

in the shade of its market stalls
i tasted your games
we were barely ten years old
and you carted your treasures
inside torn pockets

from old men on the shore
you'd steal bits of netting
to string with rocks
in the shape of seashells

with trembling hands
you left one-eyed fish
and under-ripe fruit
on my window ledge

the olive tree had a name
i'd told you in secret
along with the alphabet
they carve with flint
into the masts of ships

inventàvem l'un per l'autre
d'istòrias fantasticas
i aviá de balenas
de la lenga curiosa
i aviá tas paraulas ornadas de sal
e nòstras lagremas vertadièras
quand l'estieu trescolant
nos rendiá estrangièrs l'un a l'autre

we told one another
fantastic stories
alive with whales
who spoke a strange tongue
alive in your salt-encrusted words
and our tears were true
when the ebbing summer
made us strangers to each other

Ulisses

Te vòli retrobar dròlla
retrobar aqueles jorns de ventadas
qu'escalpravan ta cabeladura
de sabla e de sal

alara ganhavas ma cauna
dapasset
que remirèsse ta còfa
e ta mina esquèrra

parlavas pas mai
fasiás de gèstes largs
lo solelh dins ton esquina
fasiás mòure las ombras

e t'apelavi Reina

vòli engulhar mas mans de dròlle
darrièr ta nuca
portar ta cara coma un calici
e dançar coma un cèc

vòli fregar ton pé
dins la posca freda
e que ton rire me devòre

Ulysses

I want you child again
to relive the days when great winds
whipped your hair into sculptures
of sand and salt

when you came to my lair
with unhurried steps
so I'd admire your tousled crown
and peregrine bearing

you would not speak
but with grand gestures
the sun at your back
you summoned the shadows

and I called you my Queen

I want to slip the hands of a child
around the nape of your neck
to hold your face like a chalice
and sway to a blind man's dance

I want to graze your foot
in the cool dust, I want
your laughter to devour me

vòli dormir quand velhas
e que las cabras davalen lo sèrre
per anonciar la sera

te vòli veire partir e demorar sol
per reculhir
al bruch de las campanas animalas
las perlas de sabla e de sal
casudas de tos pelses

I want to sleep when you wake
as goats clatter down the hillside
to welcome the night

I want to watch you go, to be alone
when I gather
to the sound of herding bells
the salt-sand pearls
fallen from your hair

Ela

Cada nuèch lo meteis auratge
enaigava los estèus
de capelets de dròlles
crebant l'escuresa
de lors cacalasses blancs

dins ta man, servavas la meuna
aimavi ta sarrada
èras pas òme encara
mas ja promés a la guèrra
èras mon animal mainatge
ignorant lo tast del sang
e desiravi ta mossegada

She

Night after night a storm
flooded the reefs
with garlands of children
breaking through the darkness
in peals of white laughter

you took me by the hand
and i liked being held
by you, barely a man
yet already bound for war
you were my beast-child
heedless of the taste of blood
and i longed for your bite

Ulisses

Disiás « Ulisses »
dins un mormolh
al dedins de mas paumas
e passejavas ta lenga
e son perfum de figa
sus mas magras ofrendas

parlavas al futur e crenhiái aqueste baujum
la mostor sul teu front e tas velhas nuechencas
coma s'aviás servat per tu lo secret del fuòc
coma se dependiá de tu quora e a quin dieu
sacrificar la flamba

Ulysses

You whispered 'Ulysses'
a murmur
in the palm of my hand
rolling your fig-scented
tongue
over my meagre offerings

your voice dwelled in the future and I feared your madness
your fevered brow and nightly vigils
as though the secret of fire were yours to keep
and yours to decide when and to which god
the flame should yield

Chant II

L'heure est venue du premier départ.
Les garçons sont fascinés par l'éclat du métal, par les promesses des guerriers qui leur tendent la main, les appellent « fils » et mènent des bateaux grands comme des villes.

Ulysse a juré de revenir, de la prendre pour épouse.

Mais au moment de partir, Ulysse ne se retourne pas.

Canto II

The hour has come for the first parting.
The boys are mesmerized by the shine of polished metal, the promises of warriors with hands outstretched, who call them "son" and handle ships as large as cities.

Ulysses has pledged to return, to take her for his wife.

At the moment of departure, Ulysses doesn't look back.

Ela

A cada pas que vos mena
cap a las naus de tela clara
vòstras maires se foetan las cuèissas e sagnan
un second còp per vòstra pèca

lo soledre carreja lor clam luènh del ribatge
luènh de vòstres còsses tendres
luènh
cap a las tèrras
ont se creban en silenci
de cavals aganits

She

With every step you take
toward these bright-sailed vessels
your mothers whip their thighs and bleed
a second time because of you

the wind carries their lament far offshore
far from your tender bodies
far away
to lands
where in silence
emaciated horses die

Ulisses

Un gran de sabla
ta cara
maire

coma Orfèu als Infèrns
degun vos gausa portar un darrièr agach

las abelhas son nombrosas a l'entorn de nòstres pitres descobèrts
mas oblidarem deman lo tast del mel
coma avèm oblidat lo tast de vòstre lach

oblidarem que i a de sèrres
e de combas de bauca longa
e que i a d'autras colors que lo blau infinit del cèl

Ulysses

A grain of sand
your face
my mother

like Orpheus in the Underworld
none would dare cast the last glance at you

bees swarm around our naked torsos
but tomorrow we will forget the taste of honey
as we forgot the taste of your milk

we will forget there are hills
and valleys and tall grasses
and hues beyond the sky's infinite blue

Me fau de lagui pels frairòts
las èrsas ofegan lor planh
ausissèm lo mai jove que sona sa maire
mas sa votz demòra sens resson

lo ribatge dins nòstra esquina a engolida la ciutat

mas pensadas derivan cap a tu
ta votz a mon aurelha
tas labras sus mas paumas

seràs aquí a mon retorn ?

I feel for the little brothers
the surf stifles their cries
I hear the youngest call to his mother
but his voice returns no echo

the shores we left behind engulf the harbour

adrift I turn to you
your voice in my ear
your lips on the palm of my hand

will you be there when I return?

Ela

La nau que te pòrta
s'en va crebar l'orizont vuèg

alara que t'alunhas
aquí tot se retira

persistirai de fénher de pas saber
que ton astrada es sagelada
per totes aqueles cantorals
que te donaràn lors voses
e te faràn eròi
a lor imatge
e que te perdràs
dins lo tèu pròpri raconte

She

The boat that carries you
edges off to splinter the bare horizon

and as you recede in the distance
everything here melts away

i'll go on pretending i don't know
that your fate is sealed
by countless singers
who will lend you their voices
to make you a hero
in their own image
and you will lose your self
in your own story

Chant III

Elle sait de quoi sont faits les rêves d'Ulysse. La guerre, la victoire.
En récompense, que l'on se souvienne d'Ulysse.
En récompense, une île où le soleil ne se couche jamais.

Mais elle sait qu'au-delà du songe, il n'y a qu'une triste plaine envahie d'asphodèles.
Elle voudrait pouvoir y emmener Ulysse, lui dire de ne pas se perdre dans la prière, de ne pas croire aux images.

Parfois au beau milieu du jour elle allume un flambeau.
Elle imagine que tous les bateaux qui voguent sur la mer se dirigent vers elle et que dans l'un d'eux, il y a Ulysse.

Canto III

She knows what his dreams are made of. War, victory.
His reward, that Ulysses be remembered.
His reward, an island where the sun never sets.

But she knows that beyond the dream lies only a mournful plain invaded by asphodels.
She wants to lead Ulysses there, to tell him not to be fooled by prayer, not to believe the reflections.

Sometimes in broad daylight she sets a torch ablaze.
She imagines every boat that sails the sea is moving towards her and aboard one of them, sails Ulysses.

Ulisses

La còca crica
la fusta nos refusa

nos vaquí tròp brusents
tròp frèules
los frairòts gingolan
lors pupillas vènon immensas

lor englasi m'embriaga
m'inventi un sourire carnivòr
e coma se sagna l'anhèl
fenhi lo gèst del borrèu

Ulysses

The hull creaks
the timbers spurn us

we have been too loud
and too frail
the little brothers are sobbing
their pupils enormous

elated by their terror
I don a voracious grin
and mime the executioner's hand
slitting a lamb's throat

Ela

Perqué te siás pas virat ?
pr'aquò es aital qu'auriái escricha l'istòria :

« Se vira e li fa signe, ela, plora, se mossega las labras e sagna, sa man arpa son còr ma sap que tornarà e que la farà reina. »

Non
pòdi pas tot inventar
pas aital
pas
sola

She

Why did you not look back?
This is how i would have told the story:

"He looks back and waves to her, she, weeping, bites her lip till it bleeds as her hand claws at her heart though she knows he will return and make her his queen."

No
i can't just invent the whole thing
i can't
not
alone

Ulisses

Largats sus l'iscla
coma de cans dels uèlhs redonds
lutam dusca a la sang

sens pena crebariam lo frairòt
se qualque mèstre d'arma sonava pas dins una bana
quand arriba lo còp ultim

mas la mòrt es un don
lo supplici es de véncer
e sempre acarar la lutz blanca

la nuèch los uèlhs escandilhan, i a aqueles que ploran
        e aqueles que desiran
ieu vòli lo glasi, vòli lo glasi e un talh tendre ont passar
        ma carn regda

Ulysses

Let loose on an island
like wide-eyed dogs
we fight till blood is drawn

we would kill the little brother without a qualm
but for the sound of some drill-master's horn
before the fatal blow

though death is a gift
our plight is to prevail
and to brave the bleakness of the light

eyes glisten in the darkness, some with tears and some with yearning
but I want the blade, I want the blade and a tender incision
        in which to slip my rigid flesh

Ela

Vòli pas mai cantar amb las autras femnas
vòli pas d'aqueles braces flacs
e d'aqueles pièches pesucs
que cada dròlle tira sempre mai bas
vòli pas gastar ma cabeladura
jol vel de las mólhers
e veire mas mans venir rossèlas a tròp mólser d'espècias

empleni mas braietas de farina, raubi de miralhs
e compausi dins nòstra cauna
mon troçèl de femna liura

limpi, mas mans limpan, me cobrisson de farina

una sang tebesa
limpa
long de mas cuèissas

She

i don't want to sing with the women any more
i don't want their flabby arms
and heavy breasts
weighed down by children day after day
i don't want to tame my hair
with a bridal veil
or to see my hands grow sallow from grinding spices

i fill my drawers with flour, i steal mirrors
and in our grotto assemble
my free woman's trousseau

i slip, my hands slip, douse me in flour

tepid blood
seeps
down my thighs

Ulisses

Es ara temps, ça dison, de rejónher la riba

nos tustan sus l'esquina
dents defòra
nos vojan dins la garganta
una aiga qu'afisca las entralhas

es la fèsta ! nos promèton de guèrras
d'erràncias eroïcas
de pan pels poètas

mas qual son aqueles òmes
que tant de còps an sonada la trèva ?
Per de qué nos aprene la lucha ?
Per de qué sondar tantes còsses s'es pas per ne traire la vida ?

Mon punh reclama son tribut
per tota vida graciada
caldrà pagar lo dèime

Ulysses

It is time, they say, to return to shore

they strike us on the back
all teeth bared
the water they pour down our throats
warms our entrails

it's a feast! war is profferred
heroic wanderings
bread for the bards

But who are those men
who called so many truces?
Where's the sense in teaching us the art of combat?
In sounding out all these bodies, if not to take their lives?

My fist demands its rightful share
for every life spared
there's a tithe to be paid

Chant IV

Ulysse ne rêve plus que de corps à corps.

Parfois il lui semble qu'elle murmure à son oreille et lui dicte ses songes, qu'elle réclame un sacrifice, qu'Ulysse lui revienne portant trophée, du sang jusque sous les ongles.

Canto IV

The only dream Ulysses has now is of flesh wrestling with flesh.

At times it seems to him she murmurs in his ear, instructing his dreams, that she clamours for a sacrifice, for Ulysses to return to her bearing trophy, his hands drenched in blood.

Ulisses

La nau deriva sus sa pança de balena

nos desbarcan coma de marrit bestial
nos caldrà caminar puèi que sèm d'oires

las cabras lèvan lo menton
me sovèni coma se tira lo lach
de lors popas pesugas
desiri ne sasir una e beure jos la bèstia

anèm aital, en banda, de vilatge en vilatge
es estranh d'èsser ornat al biais d'un soldat
sens quitament conéisser lo tast del sang

m'agrada pas l'agachada de las vièlhas
vòli que viren los uèlhs
que se cobrissen la boca

las aimavi çaquelà, las vièlhas
sentián a comin, me cotigavan lo ventre
e servavan pel gat lo gras dels peisses

mas nos reconeisson pas o fan mina d'aver perduda la vista

Ulysses

The galley slides on its whale-smooth belly

they unload us like rank cattle
we will have to walk, since we are wineskins

the goats lift their muzzles
I remember how to draw milk
from their heavy teats
I am dying to grab one and drink straight from the beast

and so we stagger on, in gangs, from village to village
it feels strange to be rigged out like a soldier
without even knowing the taste of blood

I loathe the way the old women stare at me
I want them to avert their eyes
to cover their mouths

I did love them once, these old women
they smelled of cumin, tickled my belly
and saved scraps of fish for the cat

but they don't recognize us, else they pretend to be blind

fàcia a nòstres grands còsses adultes, nòstres còsses de traites
a lors maires
aquesta ardada de letz que manjarà lor pan e agotarà l'aiga de lor potz

avanci, serai lèu prèp de tu

i a un vilatge de mercants, de caras familiaras
de longs taulièrs que totes ofrisson la meteissa causa

i a de marins de la cabeladura sorna
se ditz que prenon las mai bèlas sens quitament las forçar

totes aqueles òmes, aquelas femnas, que demòran en rèire
de las batèstas
aqueles per quals perdrem un braç, un uèlh o la vida
o res
se ganham
e que caldrà mimar lo jòia
totes
me recòrdan aquelas bèstias
que se noirisson de la boca dels cadavres

to our full-grown bodies, bodies that betrayed their mothers
this prowling mob who will eat their bread and drain the water
    from their wells

I'm drawing close, I'll be soon by your side

there's the market town, familiar faces
long stalls each offering the same wares

there, the dark-haired seafarers
who take, they say, the most beautiful girls without even forcing them

all these men and women who stay clear of the fighting
for whom we will lose an arm, an eye, a life
or nothing
if we win
and we must feign joy
all
remind me of those animals
who feed from the mouths of the dead

Dobrissetz las fenèstras
siatz testimònis

lo solelh es riblat al zenit
la mar, al luènh, s'estira
acordada a aqueste desir alabre
que daissa mos dets blancs
quichats al margue de mon arma

i a aquí un vièlh
porgís un casco de guerrièr

me sembla lo conéisser dempuèi totjorn
qu'es demorat aquí longtemps
dins l'espèra de mon retorn

tot en el implora la desliurança
serai bon, li donarai la mòrt digna
al biais d'un soldat
e aqueste còp degun non vendrà pas sonar la trèva

« Vòls la caritat, l'aujòl ?
La caritat d'Ulisses ? »

Open your windows
and bear witness

the sun is riven to its zenith
in the distance the yawning sea
rivals a voracious appetite
that drains my knuckles white
from clenching the hilt of my sword

over there an old man
holds out a warrior's helmet

it seems I have known him forever
and he's been there a long while
waiting for me to return

everything in him cries out for deliverance
I will be kind, give him a dignified death
a soldier's death
and this time no one will call a truce

"Is it mercy you want, old man?
Mercy from Ulysses?"

pòrti lo còp al bèl mitan del ventre
la carn, lo còs tot, limpan
arrapi son casco e vesi
ma cara
bramanta
deformada
per l'òrbe del metal

d'ara enlà portarai son casco
lo portarai duscas a ma mòrt
aital me recordarai

I aim the blow at the pit of his stomach
his flesh, his entire body, slip away
I grab his helmet and I see
my face
howling
distorted
by the orb of the metal

I wear his helmet now
I will wear it until my death
to keep the memory alive

Chant V

Alors Ulysse est revenu. Il est revenu les muscles bandés et le regard sombre. Un casque luisant posé sur son crâne. Il est revenu plus beau encore que dans ses rêves à elle. Elle qui ne rêvait que de marins se hissant à pleines mains entre les cuisses de leurs femmes. Elle qui n'a jamais rêvé de sang ni de guerre ni rien désiré que d'oublier tous les récits.

Ulysse et revenu et l'un et l'autre se sont aimés. Mais il sait que le soleil a entendu ses commandements, que le soleil à tout raconté aux oiseaux et que les oiseaux murmurent à toutes les oreilles. Alors il guette.

Celle qui l'aime dort tout contre lui à même le sable.
Ulysse veille.
Il bande son arc et vise l'œil de la lune.
Quelque chose viendra et on se souviendra d'Ulysse.

Canto V

And so Ulysses returned. He returned, dark-eyed and muscle-bound. A shining helmet on his skull. He returned, ever more handsome than in her dreams. She whose dreams were of sailors hoisting themselves with cupped hands between their wives' thighs. She who had never dreamt of blood or war nor wanted anything but to forget all the stories.

Ulysses returned and they loved each other. But he knows the sun has heard his commandments, knows the sun told the birds everything and the birds in turn are whispering in every ear. And so he is watchful.

The one who loves him is asleep, curled against him on the bare sand.
Ulysses keeps watch.
He draws his bow and aims for the eye in the moon.
Something will come to pass, they will remember Ulysses.

Ela

Aital serai ta femna, luènh de tota memòria

oblidaràn lo mèu nom
n'escafarai la traça

mas en aquesta nuèch de nòças
aquesta nuèch profana
serai ta sola guida

crengas pas aqueste vertige
basta de se prene per la man
e se ronçar ensemble
al delà del voide

alara saupràs que sèm parièrs
a aquestes aucèls ferotges
percaçan lor ombra

She

And so i will be your wife, outside of memory

and my name, forgotten
i will take pains to erase any trace of it

but on this our wedding night
on this profane night
i will be your sole guide

you can't fight this vertigo
all we need do is join hands
and together leap
beyond the void

and you will see we are equal
to those fearless birds
who chase their own shadows

Ulisses

Te vesi sorire, m'as emmascat
tu que te cresès maudita a guinhar l'asuèlh
una man sus la boca e aquela trista luna rossa ficada entre tas cilhas

Ulysses

I see you are smiling, you have beguiled me
you who think yourself doomed to scan the horizon
with a hand over your mouth and that sad yellow moon stuck
        between your eyelashes

Ela

Tos uèlhs an la color d'abans l'auratge
quand res pus destria lo cèl de la mar
e que las isclas semblan de traucs dins lo miralh

es a ieu ara de portar lo còp
t'agantar per la rasiga
e te plantar dins mon còs, aquesta frucha
que pelas amb tas onglas
per ne sucar la pèl e la mastegar dapasset
abans de n'embèure lo chuc puèi de tastar la carn
trissar lo nogal, lo mesclar de saliva
entrò que n'en demòre res, res mai de ieu
levat aquel tast que demòra al dedins de ta boca

« Siás a ieu », « Soi a tu »
aital son las paraulas qu'escambian los amaires

mas te vòli pas aparténer ni desirar que siás mèu
que tu e ieu formam qu'un sol buf
una sola memòria

avèm jamai vista la man jurar fidelitat al còs ?

Te vòli aimar, Ulisses
d'un amor sobeiran

She

Your eyes are the colour of a storm before it breaks
when nothing can distinguish sky from sea
and islands seem like holes in a mirror

it's my turn to strike now
and make you take root
inside my body, inside this fruit
that you strip open with your nails
to suck its skin and slowly chew
before you soak up its juices, then savour the flesh
crush the kernel you leaven with saliva
until nothing is left, nothing other
than a taste of me that haunts your mouth

"You belong to me", "I belong to you"
such words are for lovers to share

but i don't want to be yours, i don't want to long for you to be mine
you and i are of one breath
one memory

has the hand ever sworn fealty to the body?

i want to love you, Ulysses
with a sovereign love

Ulisses

Al lindal de nòstre ostal
ai pausadas mas armas
e lo casco raubat

i aurà un viatge, una guèrra, una victòria
e un retorn

te cal me creire
mas vesi que dobtas de ieu

sabes pas que tota arma, emai la mai salvatja
a besonh d'un asil ?

Ulysses

At the threshold of our house
I lay down my weapons
and the stolen helmet

there will be voyage, war, victory
and return

I want you to trust me
but I see you doubt my word

don't you know that even the fiercest soul
hungers for asylum?

Ela

Sabi, Ulisses
sabi
mas a ton torn
Ulisses
oblides pas

oblides pas que i a d'ombras pesugas
e que se sarran, totjorn al meteis ritme
totjorn mai nombrosas
duscas a passar la riba
d'aquel cors d'aiga opac
ont poiriái negar çò que de tu es en ieu

me poiriás rejónher
o te perdre en camin

poiriái pujar dins ton batèu
me copar los pels
portar tas armas e pensar tas plagas
ofrir mon còs als morents e als soldats mai durs

o te poiriái esperar
aprene a faiçonar dins l'argela los traches de ta cara
la marcar cada jorn d'une novèla ruga
benlèu entarrar cada ser ton doble de tèrra

She

i know, Ulysses
i know
but in turn
Ulysses
do not forget

do not forget there are shadows that weigh heavy
and march on, always to the same rhythm
in ever greater numbers
to cross the shores
of this opaque waterway
where i could drown what inside me is yours

you could join me
or lose your way

i could climb aboard your ship
cut my hair
carry your weapons, dress your wounds
offer my body to the dying or to the toughest warriors

or i could wait for you
learn to fashion your features in clay
and day by day etch a new line on your face
or night after night bury this clay semblance of you

e atendre ton retorn
los braces cargats de flambèls

e se l'alba me troba sola e la cara en cendres
m'en anirai cavar ta tomba per exumar aqueste còs
qu'e m'es plan mai fisèl

and await your return
laden with torches

but should the sunrise find me, ashen-faced and alone
i will dig up your tomb and exhume this body
that is far more faithful to me

Chant VI

Ils sont venus par la mer sur de petites embarcations. Ils sont venus avec leurs barbes tressées et leurs yeux graves annoncer qu'un berger a volé une reine. Ulysse les a rejoints les armes à la main, son beau casque sur le crâne. Mais avant de partir il a prêté serment. Que son âme soit maudite s'il devait être parjure.

Il dit « retour » elle entend « départ », il dit « victoire » elle entend « solitude », il dit « à jamais », elle répond « jamais ».

Alors, les vieilles femmes ont repris le cours de leurs lamentations.
Les chiens, épouvantés, se sont rongé la croupe.
Elle s'est vêtue d'un linceul.

Canto VI

They came by sea in their small boats. They came with plaited beards and solemn eyes bearing news that a shepherd had stolen a queen. Ulysses joined them, weapons in hand, a smart helmet on his skull. But before setting off he made a pledge. May his soul be damned should he break his oath.

He says "return" she hears "departure", he says "victory" she hears "loneliness", he says "for ever" she answers "never".

And so the old women take to wailing again.
Terrified, the dogs gnaw at their rumps.
She wraps herself in a shroud.

Ulisses

Ai somiat d'el, mon enemic sul prat batalhièr

eternament parièr d'aquel costat de ma lama

nòstra solesa en comun e aquesta meteissa question

calriá poder suspendre lo temps, lo convidar a se sèire per conèisser son nom, aquel de son vilatge, saupre s'aima una femna, se recordar de sa votz, de son accent probable, emai benlèu ne rire, li ofrir un dàtil e li dostar la vida en li baisar lo front

Ulysses

I dream of him, my enemy on the battlefield

an infinite likeness from my side of the blade

our onliness shared and on the same quest

to suspend time, invite the other to sit, to learn his name, the name
of his village, to know whether he loves a woman, to remember his
voice and maybe his accent, or even laugh at it, then offer him
dates and take his life as I kiss his brow

Ela

Somias encara...

de qué somiaràs ailà sul prat batalhèr ?

i aurà lo jorn e i aurà la nuèch
dins cada camp los meteisses gèstes
gaireben una rotina
plan abans l'auròra, la teleta amb l'aiga d'una bacina
qualques pregàrias a d'estatuas austèras
fòrça, coratge, victòria

aquí s'enauça lo cant del gal

i a la batèsta, lo flus e lo reflús
plan mai de crits que necite, coma un juòc qu'auriá tròp durat
d'odors, pelses que pegan jos lo casco brausent
de còps quicòm d'intim, l'urina còsta la cuèissa al moment de morir

las cigalas exultan e puèi ven lo ser
se fa lo compte, s'engolíssan las dents, se lecan las plagas

mas demòras avugle a aquesta pantomima
segur que i a de coratge emai un sens a tot aquò

She

You're dreaming again...

what dreams will you dream, out on the battlefield?

there will be day, there will be night
in both camps, the same gestures
almost routine
well before dawn, ablutions over a basin
a few prayers to statues austere
strength, courage, victory

until cockcrow

and the battle is held, surge and counter-surge
cries, too many, as in a game gone on too long
odors, hair matted under a sweltering helmet
a trickle of urine down the thigh at the moment of death

crickets eulogize and then as darkness falls
the men take stock, swallow a few teeth, lick their wounds

but you remain blind to this masquerade
you are certain there is courage and even purpose in it all

Ulisses

Tornarai per te donar un filh

aurai coneguda la guèrra e coma se dona la mòrt
amb la ràbia sença del novèl nascut
uman udolaire, a còps de clòsca qu'a sagnat sa maire

sauprai coma se dona la mòrt, luènh dels dieuses e de tota memòria
alara que nòstre pròpri nom s'es avalit
e que las guèrras semblan tan parièras que i a pas mai de camp
sonca una dolor a tròp sarrar la maissa
lo sèxe regde quichat contra lo ventre
amb la paur d'èsser sasit aquí per la mossegada freda

Ulysses

I will return and give you a son

once I know how to wage war and give death
with the untamed rage of the howling newborn
human, head-ramming his mother till she bleeds

I'll know how to give death, far removed from the gods and from
memory itself
until our very names have deserted our mouths
and the wars seem so alike there are no sides left
only an ache from clenching our jaws too tight
a phallus stiff-pressed against the belly
and the fear of being seized by the chill of the bite

Ela

Dona-me un nom, Ulisses

dona-me un nom que te posquèsse esperar
serai aquí, i aurà lo miralh
e parlarem de tu, ieu e l'autra al dedins del miralh
la rejonharai aquí, sempre de galís, al ras d'una cadièra, al biais
dels aucèls
amb la dolor dins ma cuèissa per me pas perdre d'aquel costat del
miralh

lo matin portarai mos pendents d'aurelhas
los servarai emai benlèu al lièch se me deviás susprene al mitan
de la nuèch

mas s'ai pas de nom cossi saupre quala d'entre ela o ieu velha ?

She

Give me a name, Ulysses

give me a name so that i can wait for you
i'll be here, the mirror, there
and we'll speak of you, i and the other in the mirror
i'll join her there, a little slant, on the edge of a chair,
            the way birds do
the ache in my thigh keeps me from losing myself to that side
            of the mirror

in the morning i'll wear my earrings
i may even wear them to bed should you surprise me in the night

but if i have no name how will i know which of us, her or me,
            is waiting?

Ulisses

Te donar un nom ?

Te donar un nom quand balas dins lo negre dins de carrièras desèrtosas
amb de grands gosses ?

Te donar un nom quand vas a la rivièra en tenguda de nuèch jos lo
naut solelh en ignorar los òmes que se son perduts
en te cresent sasir ?

T'ofrirai d'iranges
e per las pelar un cotèl pas mai grand que lo poce
un cotèl d'ivòri qu'aurai raubat aprèp la batalha
lo present d'un defunt a una autra femna
e te caldrà pensar a ela, a sos lençòls freds, al trauc dins sa pòcha
a la plaça del cotèl

t'ofrirai de brots d'èrbas qu'aurai servats longtemps jos ma sòla
que creisson aquí ont repausan los còsses
e se quilhan coma de sentinelas al quite punt ont s'acaba la fugida

Ulysses

Give you a name?

Give you a name when you dance in the dark with great hounds in
empty streets?

Give you a name when you stroll to the river dressed in your
night gown under the glaring sun, spurning the lost men
who believed they possessed you?

I'll offer you oranges
and to peel them a knife no bigger than a thumb
an ivory knife I'll steal when the battle is over
a dead man's gift to another woman
and you'll be bound to think of her, of her cold sheets, of the hole
in her pocket traded for the knife

I'll offer you blades of grass that cling to the soles of my feet
from shoots that grow there, where the bodies lie
standing tall as sentinels at the precise point their retreat
was cut short

Chant VII

Il y eut un homme. Il y eut une femme.
Puis de mémoire d'hommes, il y eut un mythe.

Le Récit débute au premier jour de la bataille
et se poursuit par les chemins humides sur la trajectoire du retour.

Il y aura de nouveaux hommes et de nouveaux récits.
De nouveaux récits à la mémoire d'un homme qui s'appelait Ulysse.

Canto VII

There was a man. There was a woman,
And after, within living memory, a myth was born.

The Tale begins on the first day of battle and follows the waterways of its return trajectory.

There will be other men and other stories.
Other tales to the memory of a man named Ulysses.

Ela

Me vaquí sola un còp de mai
amb aquela pluèja fina que s'encapricia a tot acordar
a tirar une armonia d'aquel païsatge aissable

Ulisses es partit

lo spectacle es acabat
avèm barrats los prèstamorres dins la cava
amb las cortinas

aquí lo poèta raia...
caldriá qu'una femna espère Ulisses
una femna, un can
e d'òmes
que tot a l'entorn la cortejan

She

i am here, alone again
with this soft rain that insists on blending everything together
on finding harmony in this hateful landscape

Ulysses exits

the stage is deserted
the extras are consigned to the cellar
along with the set

the poet crosses this out...
what's missing is a woman to wait for Ulysses
a woman, a dog
and men
to surround and to court her

Tot sembla contrit

lo solelh
voide

ieu ai bastit un laberint pel solèlh
i a un taure
mas pas aqueste, non
un brau rosset, los uèlhs coma de bilhas
es el, lo solelh – paura bestiòta cèga

e se lo solelh cantava
los aucèls, lors alas serián tot brutladas

It all seems chastened

the sun
void

i built a labyrinth for the sun
there's a bull
no, not that one
a small rust-tinged bull, with eyes like marbles
he's the sun, poor little blind beast

and if the sun should sing
the birds, their wings would burn to cinders

I a tota mena de tristum

i a l'aiga que raja d'aquesta grasala de malur
las alisadas que nos impausa lo gèst
lo plaser intacte de l'aiga tebesa
e se daissam anar a trobar polida la lutz
que l'aiga captura
pivelar per las botiòlas
emai se i a de lagremas e que cason
las botiòlas, la tebesor, las rafiduras sul dessus de las mans
tot aquò impausa una atura

aquí, òc
una atura

mas ton nom me tòrna
e me voldriái enterrar amb l'aiga de mon banh

There are all manner of sorrows

water pouring from this damned basin
caresses ordained by the gesture
the perennial pleasure of warm water
letting yourself be captured
in the way that water catches the light
finding rapture in bubbles
even as the tears, the tears are falling
bubbles, warmth, creases on the back of my hand
all calling for a truce

here, now
a truce

but your name comes back to me
and i want to bury myself in this pool of water

Pòrti un braçalet a cada pé
cal dire que fau un pauc coma vòli
pas d'òme, pas de nom, pas de filh
aquí tota sola, soi la reina

òc, m'apelava aital, Ulisses
aquò's quicòm per ieu
es un pauc tot çò que soi, la reina
es aquela qu'a la paraula
a un rei
es sovent luènh amb de cavals
non, pas los cavalons de la montanha
non, de cavals grandasses raubats a de peirièrs
amb de bravas maissas e lo còl solid aquí ont es plantat lo cap

vaquí
las parets son nautas
se dança a son entorn mas ela dança pas jamai

i a pas de musica, pas de votz fòra de la meuna
i a ben lo miralh mas ai mentit, m'i vòli pas veire
benlèu, lo virar cap al cèl
o un bèl jorn partir
e lo plantar aquí, ben fàcia a la pòrta

i wear a bracelet on each ankle
you could say i do more or less as i please
no man, no name, no son
alone as i am, i am the queen

yes, that's what he used to call me, Ulysses
that's my lot
she's sort of all me, the queen
the one whose turn it is to speak
she has a king
he's often far from home, with his horses
no, not the little mountain horses
no, tall horses they took from the stonemasons
with massive jaws and thick necks to bear the weight of their heads

there it is
the walls are steep
dancing surrounds her, but she will not dance

there is no music, no voice other than mine
yes, i do have a mirror but i lied, i don't want to see myself in it
i may turn it towards the sky
or take my leave one day
and prop it there, staring straight at the door

E tu, qual sès?

Non pas Ulisses, non
es luènh, Ulisses
que s'estaque plan a son aure...

Qual sès tu? De qué as somiat aquesta nuèch ?
Sès òme o femna ?
As un nom, solide, de parents
es probable que siás ni avugle ni mai sord
mas benlèu malaut ?

Non, o sèm totes, non, desmembra aquel glacet dins la peitrina
ne sèm totes aquí
avèm de pressentidas, puèi se passa pas res
o quicòm passa
e es ja tròp tardièr

And you, who are you?

No, not Ulysses
he's far at sea, Ulysses
let him cling to the mast of his ship...

You, who are you? What did you dream of last night?
Are you man, are you woman?
You have a name, that much is certain, parents
yo may not be blind nor deaf
but are you ailing?

No, we all are, no, forget the ice in your chest
everyone is stranded here
we all have premonitions though nothing comes to pass
or else something does
and by then it's too late

Ieu aniriái plan al prèp d'Ulisses amb las serenas
e li demandarai perqué las serenas semblan tant las arpías

es benlèu per aquò qu'un jorn, lor talharem las alas ?
Perque aurai pausada aquesta question...

Es benlèu ma fauta
se de drolletas
se negan dins de lacs
en voler jogar a las serenas

aquò poncha los uèlhs, la baudra

i'd rather join Ulysses amongst the sirens
i could ask him why sirens resemble harpies so

perhaps their wings are yet to be clipped?
Because i would have asked...

am i to blame i wonder
for little girls
who drown in lakes
pretending to be sirens

stung by the mire in their eyes

Mas non, t'en fagas pas
i a res que se posquèsse pas dire
perque sèm
aquí
ara

coma cadun de nautres te siás demandat
— e aprèp ?

Aprèp ? res, pas res
es pas pasible

But no, let it be
there is nothing to be said
because we're
here
now

With everyone, you wonder
—*what next?*

Next? nothing, nothing at all
it isn't peaceful.

Esta, te vau contar una istòria :

m'an donat una cabreta
dormi amb ela de còps contra un arbre o contra una paret
senti dins mon esquina lo contact raspós de la rusca o de la peira seca
mas aquesta dolor flaquís
se retira dins la claror de sos sòmis

coma sempre dins mos recòrds, es mièjjorn
coma sempre, ai tretze ans

jògi amb lo mèu fraire
cadun ten un tròç del miralh cap al plafón
caminam cauta-cauta
en tot encambar los traus d'aqueste membre unenc qu'es nòstre ostal
a la debuta avèm lo vertigi e puèi aquò passa
avançam en silenci cap al lindal
e cabussam dins la gorga del cèl

es mièjjorn, lo potz es dubèrt
a cregut poder corrér sus aquela paret
coma sus los bauces nautes de sos sòmis de cabra

es mièjjorn
e lo solelh a flor d'aiga s'es trencat

Hush now, let me tell you a story:

i was given a little she-goat.
i sometimes sleep next to her against a tree or wall
i feel the roughness of bark or hard rock on my back
but the ache soon eases
eclipsed in the brightness of her dreams

as ever in this memory, it is noon
as ever, i'm thirteen

i am playing with my brother
together we hold a mirror to the ceiling
cautiously we begin
to step over the rafters of this single room that is our house
at first we are dizzy but then it passes
we move in silence toward the entrance
and dive headlong into the depth of the sky

it is noon, the well is open
she thought she could scramble up its wall
just like the steep cliffs of her she-goat dreams

it is noon
and the sun has broken at the water's surface

A de moments parièrs, oblidi gaireben qu'Ulisses es aquí tanben

mas dins aquel païsatge, i a pas que de parets

ausisses, Ulisses ?

Poirás mila còps gaitar en rèire
cambiar de votz e de cara
aqueste territòri es pas pro vast per que se perde lo resson
de nòstras paraulas

It happens now and then, i almost forget that Ulysses, too, is here

but in this land all i see are walls

do you hear, Ulysses?

You may look back a thousand times
change your voice and appearance
this land is not vast enough to dispel the echo of our words

Me senti venir vièlha

sabi pas res mai de tu, Ulisses

de totes los òmes que son partits a la guèrra, comptan sonca
los mòrts
m'an res dich de tu, alara sabi qu'endacòm sès plan viu

benlèu que i a una trèva, e mai benlèu siás partit pescar
e per un còp es un pauc coma abans
al cap d'una canavèra as trenat lo crin d'un caval
as pensat a ieu, as retrobat los gèstes candes
lo ponh brausent al contact de la rema, la sal sus ta cara
te siás ausit rire
e puèi a aqueles que sabon pas, mòstras coma se voida lo peis
las mans claufidas d'escaumas, benlèu que tenès aquel cotèl
que servas per ieu ?
auriatz l'agach solombrós al moment de fendre la carn grisa
i auriá qualque tremolums, una part invesibla dins cada gèst

que podètz pas far coma se saviatz pas
que la guèrra es un juòc que vòstra vida n'es la mesa
e que serà totjorn tròp d'ora per quitar la partida

As i grow old

i hear no more about you, Ulysses

but of all the men who've gone to war, we only count the dead
no one has brought me word of you, and so i know that somewhere
you are alive

was there a truce, or did you go fishing, for once a little like old times
at the tip of a reed you braided a strand of horse hair
and thought of me, remembering those simple gestures
the burn of your fist on the oar, the salt on your face
you heard yourself laugh
and now to those who don't know how, you teach the art
of gutting fish
your hands covered in scales, do you use the knife you saved for me?
your eyes grow dim as you split the grey flesh
there is a tremor, a thing unseen in every gesture

you can't go pretending you didn't know
that war is a game, and your life its wager
and it's always too soon to quit the fray

Soi lassa de tirar un per un los fials blancs que teissons las sasons
dins ma cabeladura
e puèi i a aquelas tascas sus l'esquina de mas mans
las sèrvi d'ara enlà dins los plecs de ma tunica, a cobèrt

en dedins tanben, senti plan que tot se fendascla

aimariái èsser de gèis per poder remendar tot aquò
un pauc d'aiga e de tèrra
e vaquí, seriái parièra a ton recòrd
liça, urosa
e plena encara de tu

i'm tired of teasing out white threads the seasons have braided
through my hair
and there are spots on the back of my hands
i keep them hidden now in the folds of my tunic

on the inside too, i feel every crack

i wish i were made of clay, so i could repair these things
a little water, a little earth
and i'd soon be as you remember me
smooth, serene
and still sated with you

Ai tot reinventat
cadun de tos retorns
tas paraulas
tas alisadas

de còps intravas dins aquesta pèça e te limpavas contra ieu alara
    que somiavi
de còps lo rebotge dels cans me daissava creire que veniás per la rota
e tota vela dins l'asuèlh me semblava èsser sonca la teuna

ai tròp somiat, Ulisses, t'ai tròp esperat

ne pòdi pas mai de totas las conjecturas que m'impausa la volada
    dels aucèls
ne pòdi pas mai d'aqueste destin de Moera
barrar las fenèstras, dormir pel sòl
e gemegar entrò que me brande la garganta
o que ma pròpria torpor m'assole

tota aquesta pena m'es tant familiara
que comenci de la presar

soi benlèu jamai estada tant pròche de tu que dempuèi que t'espèri

agacha-me, Ulisses
agacha plan çò qu'as fach de ieu

i reinvented every moment
every homecoming
your words
your caresses

at times you enter this room and slip in beside me as i sleep
at times i imagine the restless dogs announce your arrival by road
and every sail on the horizon is yours

too many dreams, Ulysses, i've waited too long

i can no longer bear reading signs into the flights of birds
i can't bear the burden of the Fates
drawing the curtains, sleeping on the ground
and wailing until fire seizes my throat
or i find solace in my own torpor

all this pain is so intimate
i begin to cherish it

and it seems i have never been closer to you than in this waiting

look at me, Ulysses
and see what you have done to me

Ulisses
ton
nom
es
un
blasfèmi

e ton amor un dieu d'exili

Ulysses
your
name
is
blasphemy

and your love, a god of exile

Chant VIII

Sur le chemin du retour, Ulysse a compté ses pas.
La maison est vide, le toit a brûlé. Les chaises, la table et le lit ont les quatre pieds tournés vers le trou dans le plafond.
Autour tout est identique.
Pris de panique, il a songé à compter à rebours.
Et comme il est écrit dans les livres, Ulysse a pleuré.

De retour au pays, sur le bord de la route, Ulysse veille.
Chaque matin et chaque soir, il se lave les dents, peigne sa barbe blanche, frotte avec soin son casque de métal. Ulysse ne rêve plus.

Ulysse a deux ombres. L'une immobile, projetée par un soleil visqueux, se tasse sous son corps et, à certaines heures, en marge. L'autre, vibrante, jeune encore et qui grandit, rêve plus qu'elle ne veille et rêve d'être immense, d'inspirer aux sculpteurs l'image de la victoire. Cette ombre-là dérive quelque part au large, viendra bientôt s'échouer dans les eaux basses.

Mais il est dit qu'un même homme ne peut avoir deux ombres car il n'existe au pays des mangeurs de pain qu'un seul soleil et qu'une seule lune.

Canto VIII

On his way home, Ulysses counted his steps.
The house is empty, the roof a burned-out shell. The chairs, table and bed upturned, legs pointing to the hole in the ceiling.
All around, everything remains unchanged.
Panic-stricken, he wanted to count backwards.
And as is written in the books, Ulysses wept.

Back home, by the road, Ulysses waits.
Morning and evening, he brushes his teeth, combs his white beard and shines his metal helmet with care. Ulysses no longer dreams.

Ulysses has two shadows. One, motionless, projected by a viscous sun, squats under his body, and, at certain times of day, to the side. The other, vibrant, still young and growing, dreams instead of waiting, and it dreams of being immense, of inspiring in sculptors a vision of victory. That shadow is adrift somewhere on the open sea, will soon run aground in the shallows.

But they say one man cannot have two shadows, for in the land of bread-eaters there are but one sun and one moon.

Ulisses

Me sembla qu'ai de tot temps caminat
coma s'èri sortit d'aplomb del ventre de ma maire

ausissi pas mai ta votz
alara fau lo compte de mos passes
prèni una pausa
me sièti, me lequi los dets
e fau tornamai lo compte de mos passes

te vodi cadun de mos sòmis
mas que sómie o que velhe
ausissi pas mai ta votz

ai onorada ma paraula pertant
ai presa la rota al tèrme de la batèsta

tu que pretendiás conéisser totes los endemans
deuriás saupre que i aguèt un naufragi
que mos companhs son mòrts

alara perqué venes pas cap a ieu
los braces cargats de flambèls
me mostrar lo camin ?

Ulysses

It seems I have been walking for ever
as if I had emerged upright from my mother's womb

I cannot hear your voice now
and so I count my steps
I take my rest
I sit down, lick my fingers
again I count my steps

I devote every one of my dreams to you
yet come sleep or waking
I can't hear your voice any more

even though I kept my word
I took to the road after the battle ended

you, who claim to be versed in every tomorrow
ought to know there was a shipwreck
and my companions are dead

so why don't you come to me now
laden with torches
and show me the way?

Sauprai fugir ton silenci
me crebarai los ausidors
amb aqueste cotèl raubat a un òme qu'ai quitament pas tuat
e a una femna que benlèu l'aurà pas plorat
se serà ronçada dins la jaça d'un vivent
perque la nuèch es grisa e que tot se sembla
e que çò mai penible, veses, es pas de demembrar
    mas de téner paraula

I know how to elude your silence
I'll pierce my eardrums
with the tip of this knife stolen from a man I didn't kill
from a woman who may not have mourned for him
but rushed into bed with the living
because the night is grey and it all looks the same
and the hardest thing, you see, isn't to forget, but to keep your word

Sus ma rota, ai trobat un miralh

e dedins un aujòl

li ai talhat los pelses, rasat la barba, netejat las onglas

e me soi tornat metre lo casco

On the road, I found a mirror

and in the mirror an old man

I cut his hair, shaved his beard, scrubbed his nails

and reached for my helmet again

Agacha-me

soi coma aqueles cans perduts
que bordejan las parets de las vilas
en quista d'una cara

me traison de pan d'en naut de las fenèstras
lo sèrvi dins ma boca, lo fau durar
que se mescle a ma saliva, que se dissòlve
amb la vergonha d'aquel que fa l'almòina

Look at what I have become

I am like those stray dogs
hugging the town walls
in search of a face

they throw me scraps of bread from the windows above
I turn them over in my mouth, make the bread last
let it melt in my saliva, let it dissolve
and with it my shame at taking alms

Se sembla que lo meteis arquitecta a tornat bastir totes los vilatges

aiman mai saupre pas de que ne còsta
celebrar los eròis
aqueles que son plan mòrts

mas se sap pas que far
d'aqueles que s'obstinan sul camin del retorn
e seguisson las auras caudas dels vèspres de caumaci

The same architect has rebuilt all the villages, it seems

they would rather not know the cost
let them celebrate the heroes
the ones who are truly dead

but they don't know what to do
with those who linger by the roadside on the way home
tracking warm winds on heat-ridden nights

Çò que vèsi
al tèrme de ma marcha
me daissa creire
que me soi enganat de camin
o que soi un autre
un forastièr descauç
aquel vièlh òme que plora
dins lo quadre d'una pòrta

The sight that greets me
at journey's end
leads me to believe
I took a wrong turn
or I am another
stranger in bare feet
some old man weeping
in the frame of a doorway

Es doncas aital ?

Me condemnas
a demorar sus lindal
e me clavelar lo còs ?

Pensavi que seriás aquí, que m'esperariás
que lo temps seriá pas comptat

t'auriái aimada emai vièlha, t'auriái aimada encara mai
auriái aimat tas popas magras e los plecs de tas ancas
t'auriái penchenada e convencuda que tota aquesta blancor
es aquesta de las divessas escarlpradas dins lo marbre

auriái aimat tot aquò
e ta votz novèla
e tot parièr ton còs

Is this how it's to be?

You, sentencing me
to remain at the threshold
my body transfixed?

I thought you would be here, would wait for me
that the days would not be counted

I would have loved you, old as you are, I would have loved you
all the more
I would have loved your sunken breasts and the folds of your waist
I would have combed your hair, convinced you that white
is the blush of a marble-hewn goddess

I would have loved all of you
your newfound voice
as much as your body

Mas sias pas aquí
me daissas sol amb mas victòrias
lo raconțe de la batèsta e aquel del retorn
me daissas sol
acarat a aqueste miralh
que penja sul voide

Compreni ara ton absència
ton silenci
aqueste païsatge de galís
aquesta dolor dins mas cuèissas
a cada pas perdut sus aqueste travèrs del mond

But you are not here
you have left me to my victories
to my tale of battle and my tale of return
you have left me alone
facing the mirror
that leans into the void

I understand now
your silence
this oblique landscape
the ache that grips my thighs
with every stray step on this side of the world

Vau doncas demorar aquí
apeyat contra la murâlha, al mai pròche de la rota

aquí ont tos pès an daissat un cròs dins lo sòl
aquí ont m'as esperat cada jorn amb una frucha
qu'auriam partida per festejar mon retorn
e que te daissava creire que mon retorn èra pròche

sias demorada aquí, longtemps, amb de fruchas puèi de granas
qu'as donadas a la fin als aucèls

e coma una gacha qu'a comprés que la guèrra se tendrà pas
e que la relèva vendrà pas mai
as barrada la pòrta de ta cèla, tracha la clau per la fenèstra
e dessenhat sus totas las parets
un cèl semblable a aquel de l'enfància

And so I will stay, outside the village gate
and lean against the stone wall, nearest the road

here, where your feet left their imprint on the ground
here, where you waited day after day with fruit
we would share in the joy of finding each other again
hoping this offering would bode my imminent return

here you remained a long time, with some fruit then with seeds
you ended up scattering for the birds

and like the watchman who has understood there will be no war
no changing of the guards
you locked your cell door
threw the key from your window
and painted a childhood sky on every wall

Epilogue

Elle

Allons, Ulysse, ouvre les yeux !

Tu connais les détails du décor...

C'est l'heure la plus chaude
la route est déserte
les arbres paraissent vieillis
et les toits plus luisants

le jeune soldat qui vient à ta rencontre
est en tout point identique
à la dernière image que j'ai gardée de toi

il avance tête nue et tu lui offres ton casque

son ombre se précipite, glisse jusqu'à la tienne
son ombre s'apprête à retrouver son gîte
quand il se penche et te murmure

« Tu veux la charité, vieillard ?
La charité d'Ulysse ? »

She

Come now, Ulysses, open your eyes!

You know every last detail of the set...

It's the hottest time of day
the road is deserted
the trees appear to have aged
and the roofs gleam more intently

the young soldier approaching
is the very likeness of you
when i saw you last

he greets you bare-headed, so you offer your helmet

his shadow rushes in, slips into yours
his shadow is ready to re-enter its lair
when he leans in close to murmur

"Is it mercy you want, old man?
Mercy from Ulysses?"

Tu vois ?
L'éternité existe
laissons-la porter ton masque
laissons-la se souvenir d'Ulysse

Do you see?
Eternity is real
let her wear your mask
let her remember Ulysses

Pourvu que tu me rejoignes
en marge de la mémoire
à l'heure bleue
dans le repli des vagues

And you may find me still
on the edge of memory
at the blue hour
in the fold of a wave

The Poet

Aurélia Lassaque (b. 1983) is a bilingual poet who composes in French and Occitan, the language of the medieval troubadours. She is a leading contemporary voice in Occitan and her work has been translated into a dozen languages. She is the author of several collections including: *Shadows of the Moon; Solstice, the Call of Janus;* and *For the Salamanders to Sing.* A previous book of her work in English, *Solstice and Other Poems,* was published in 2012. She lives in the village of Autoire in the south of France.

The Translator

Madeleine Campbell is a freelance translator and transdisciplinary researcher at Edinburgh University (Scotland). Her translations of Francophone Maghrebi poets have been anthologized and have appeared in several magazines. Her translations from this collection have appeared in *Poetry at Sangam*, on the Poetry International Festival website (Rotterdam), in *Poems from the Edge of Extinction* and *The Arkansas International* (2020). Her translation of Lassaque's short story 'Whalesong' appeared in *Asymptote* (2020). Madeleine's edited books on intersemiotic and experiential translation challenge traditional notions of literary translation through the embodied perspective of practitioners working in a range of media.

Author's Acknowledgments

Some of these poems were previously published:

Books:

Lassaque, A. (Forthcoming). Excerpts from *In Search of a Face,* (M. Campbell, Trans.). In Priya Sarukkai Chabria and Mrinalini Harchandrai (Eds.) *The Dragon's Heart: World Poetry in Translation.* Jadavpur University Press.

Lassaque, A. (2019). 'Ela/She'. In Chris McCabe (Ed.), *Poems from the Edge of Extinction.* (M. Campbell, Trans.). pp. 218-219. London: Chambers.

Magazines:

Lassaque, A. (2020). Excerpts from *In Search of a Face.* (M. Campbell, Trans.). *The Arkansas International.* Issue 9. www.arkint.org/aurelia-lassaque

Webpages:

www.odyssey.pm/contributors/aurelia-lassaque/

www.poetryinternational.com/en/poets-poems/poet/102-29125_Lassaque

I would like to express my heartfelt gratitude to Madeleine Campbell for her insightful translation, her patience, and her attention to detail, as well as for the memory of that first passionate conversation at the Stanza Festival in St Andrews, Scotland. I am also deeply thankful to Eleanor Livingstone, the festival's director at the time, for making this encounter possible.

I extend my sincere thanks to Clive Boutle, the first publisher who gave me the confidence to publish my poems in English, with the dedication and talent of James Thomas.

My gratitude also goes to the remarkable and flamboyant poet, my dear friend Tzveta Sofronieva, for her complicity, friendship, and our poetic sisterhood.

I am profoundly grateful to Steve Bradbury, my companion on this translation journey since 2017. Steven, who, in the first days of 2025, created the illustration for this book's cover, and thanks to whom I had the immense joy of discovering the island of Taiwan—its landscapes, its native languages, and its poets.

Finally, I would like to extend my warmest thanks to Dennis Maloney and Elaine LaMattina, as well as the entire team at White Pine Press, for this extraordinary work, which marks the beginning of a new chapter in Ulysses' adventures.

Forthcoming in 2025:

Un autre monde que le mien, Editions Bruno Doucey, Paris; as editor: *L'ombre messagère et autres moissons de poèmes*, a poetry anthology of the Occitan poet Max Rouquette published by Editions Bruno Doucey; as translator: *Les naufragés du Désert*, Zingonia Zingone, published by La Rumeur Libre Editions.

Translator's Acknowledgments

"I extend my warmest thanks to Aurélia Lassaque for entrusting me with the task of translating her beautiful bilingual collection En quête d'un visage. I am deeply indebted to ALTA for their mentorship award in 2017 and special thanks to ALTA mentor Steve Bradbury for his generous feedback and suggestions in the process of translating this collection. Finaly, my heartfelt thanks to Dennis Maloney and White Pine Press for enabling wider readership through the publication of this entire collection in the English language."

Cliff Becker Book Prize in Translation

> "Translation is the medium through which American readers gain greater access to the world. By providing us with as direct a connection as possible to the individual voice of the author, translation provides a window into the heart of a culture."
>
> —Cliff Becker, May 16, 2005

Cliff Becker (1964–2005) was the National Endowment for the Arts Literature Director from 1999 to 2005. He began his career at the NEA in 1992 as a literature specialist, was named Acting Director in 1997, and in 1999 became the NEA's Director of Literature.

The publication of this book of translation is a reflection of Cliff's passionate belief that the arts must be accessible to a wide audience and not subject to vagaries of the marketplace. During his tenure at the NEA, he expanded support for individual translators and led the development of the NEA Literature Translation Initiative. His efforts did not stop at the workplace, however. He carried his passion into the kitchen as well as into the board room. Cliff could often be seen at home relaxing in his favorite, worn-out, blue T-shirt, which read, "Art Saves Me!" He truly lived by this credo.

To ensure that others got the chance to have their lives impacted by uncensored art, Cliff hoped to create a foundation to support the literary arts which would not be subject to political changes or fluctuations in patronage, but would be marked solely for the purpose of supporting artists, and in particular, the creation and distribution of art which might not otherwise be available. While he could not achieve this goal in his short life, seven years after his untimely passing, his vision was realized.

The Cliff Becker Endowment for the Literary Arts was established by his widow and daughter in 2012 to give an annual publication prize in translation in his memory. The Cliff Becker Book Prize in Translation annually produces one volume of literary translation in English. It is our hope that with ongoing donations to help grow the Becker Endowment for the Literary Arts, important artists will continue to touch, and perhaps save, the lives of those whom they reach through the window of translation.

Donations to The Cliff Becker Endowment for the Literary Arts will help ensure that Cliff 's vision continues to enrich our literary heritage.

In Search of a Face - Aurelia Lassaque. Translated by Madeleine Campbell, 2025.

Notes from the Sea - Marjorie Agosín. Translated by Suzanne Jill Levine. 2024.

Memory Rewritten - Mariella Nigro. Translated by Jesse Lee Kercheval and Jeannine Marie Pitas, 2023.

The Beginning of Water - Le Khanh. Translated by the author and Bruce Weigl, 2021.

Hatchet - Carmen Boullosa. Translated by Lawrence Schimel, 2020.

Bleeding from All 5 Senses - Mario Santiago Papasquiaro. Translated by Cole Heinowitz, 2019.

The Joyous Science: Selected Poems - Maxim Amelin. Translated by Derek Mong and Anne O. Fischer, 2018.

Purifications or the Sign of Retaliation - Myriam Fraga. Translated by Chloe Hill, 2017.

Returnings: Poems of Love & Distance - Rafael Alberti. Translated by Carolyn L. Tipton, 2016.

The Milk Underground - Ronny Someck. Translated by Hana Inbar and Robert Manaster, 2015.

Selected Poems of Mikhail Yeryomin. Translated by J. Kates, 2014.

A Hand Full of Water - Tzveta Sofronieva. Translated by Chantel Wright, 2012.